Searchlight
BOOKS™

Do You Dig
Earth Science?

Researching

Rocks

Sally M. Walker

Lerner Publications Company
Minneapolis

Lerner Publications Company
A division of Lerner Publishing Group, Inc.
241 First Avenue North
Minneapolis, MN 55401 U.S.A.

Website address: www.lernerbooks.com

Library of Congress Cataloging-in-Publication Data

Walker, Sally M.
    Researching rocks / by Sally M. Walker.
        pages   cm — (Searchlight books™—Do you dig earth science?)
    Includes index.
    ISBN 978-1-4677-0018-4 (lib. bdg. : alk. paper)
    1. Rocks—Juvenile literature. I. Title.
QE432.2.W3439 2013
522—dc23   2012017606

Manufactured in the United States of America
1 – PC – 12/31/12

Contents

Chapter 1

WHAT IS A ROCK?

Rocks are everywhere you look. Mountains made of rock point at the sky. And rocks rattle and roll across the ground. A rock can be bigger than a house. Or it can be tiny, like a grain of sand on a beach.

Most of Earth is made of rock. What is Earth's rocky outer layer called?

Earth's Crust

Sheets of rock lie just beneath Earth's soil and water. These sheets of rock are called Earth's crust. The crust is Earth's outer layer. Most of the inside of Earth is made of rock too.

MOST OF THE ROCKS WE SEE ARE PIECES THAT HAVE BROKEN OFF OF EARTH'S CRUST.

Minerals

Rocks are made of minerals. A mineral is a solid substance that is not alive. Minerals form inside Earth. More than thirty-five hundred different kinds of minerals are found on Earth.

Some minerals are soft. Talc is a soft mineral. You could scratch it with your fingernail. Some baby powder is made of ground-up talc.

Talc is very soft. Any other mineral can scratch it.

Other minerals are hard. Quartz is a hard mineral. You would have to hit quartz with a hammer to break it. Diamond is the hardest mineral of all. A hard mineral can scratch any softer mineral. So diamond can scratch any other mineral.

Minerals can be many different colors. A rock gets its color from the minerals it's made of.

Most quartz is clear, like glass. Purple quartz is called amethyst.

Chapter 2

IGNEOUS ROCKS

All rocks on Earth belong to one of three groups. Igneous rocks are one group. Igneous rocks are made deep inside Earth, where it is very hot. It is so hot that rocks melt!

Pumice rock is full of holes. Pumice is made from melted rock. What do we call melted rock that is inside Earth?

Magma

Melted rock inside Earth is called magma. Magma isn't solid. Instead, it is soft, like toothpaste or thick syrup. Magma doesn't stay in one place. It moves around inside Earth. It pushes up toward Earth's surface. It squeezes into cracks in hard rock.

Melted rock is thick and gooey.

When melted rock cools, it becomes hard.

Earth's crust is much cooler than magma. So hot magma cools when it moves into the crust. The magma changes into solid rock. The cooled magma has become igneous rock.

Lava

Sometimes magma flows out of holes in Earth's crust. The holes are called volcanoes. The magma spills out onto Earth's surface. Then the melted rock is called lava. Very hot lava is bright orange and yellow. As it flows across the ground, it looks like a fiery river. Lava's color becomes darker and darker as it cools. When lava gets cool enough, it becomes solid. It turns into igneous rock.

Hot lava glows red, orange, or yellow. This lava is flowing out of a volcano in Hawaii.

Lava oozes from cracks along the ocean floor too. Cold seawater quickly cools the lava. Sometimes the lava hardens into round, pillow-shaped rocks.

Round lumps of hardened lava are called pillow lava because they look sort of like pillows.

Crystals in Rocks

As melted rock cools, the minerals it is made of may form crystals. Crystals are solid shapes. They have many flat surfaces. Each flat surface is called a face. Some igneous rocks have many flat, shiny bits in them. The shiny bits are crystal faces.

It takes time for a crystal to form. When a crystal begins to form, it is very tiny. Slowly, the crystal grows bigger.

These crystals have many long, narrow faces.

Sometimes melted rock cools slowly. Other times, melted rock cools quickly. Crystals can help you figure out whether a rock cooled slowly or quickly.

Some igneous rocks have large crystals. What does that tell you? It tells you that these rocks cooled slowly. The crystals had a lot of time to grow.

IT TOOK A WHILE FOR THESE LARGE CRYSTALS TO GROW.

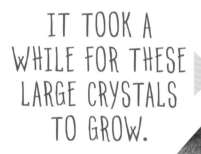

Other igneous rocks have tiny crystals. Can you guess what that means? It means that these rocks cooled more quickly. The crystals did not have time to grow big.

Some igneous rocks have no crystals at all. They cooled so quickly that crystals didn't have time to start growing.

Obsidian is a kind of igneous rock. It is as smooth as glass with no crystals at all. Do you think obsidian forms when lava cools slowly or quickly?

Chapter 3

SEDIMENTARY ROCKS

Sedimentary rocks are the second group of rocks. Sedimentary rocks form on Earth's surface or just beneath it.

Some rocks are made of small pieces of mud, sand, or stones. What are these pieces called?

Sediments

Sedimentary rocks are made of small pieces called sediments. Some sediments are bits of mud, sand, or small stones. Other sediments are shells or pieces of bone. When sediments harden together, they become sedimentary rock.

Wind and rain can break tiny pieces off large rocks. The pieces are sediments. You can see piles of sediments at the bottom of this rocky cliff.

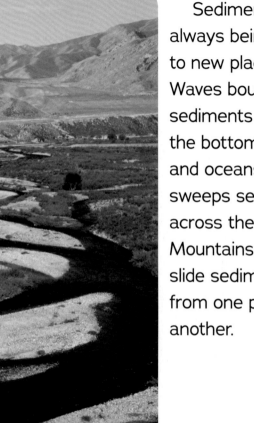

Sediments are always being moved to new places. Waves bounce sediments along the bottom of rivers and oceans. Wind sweeps sediments across the land. Mountains of ice slide sediments from one place to another.

When water in a river slows down, it can no longer carry sediments with it. The sediments fall to the bottom. Sometimes the sediments form big piles.

Sediments pile up to form a layer. A layer of sediments can be on the land. Or it can be underwater.

A SAND DUNE IS SAND
THAT HAS BEEN BLOWN
INTO A PILE BY THE WIND.

Heavy Layers

New layers of sediments form on top of older ones. Sometimes the layers of sediments are different colors. If you could cut through the layers, they would look like stripes.

Sediment layers can be thousands of feet thick. Deep layers of sediments are heavy. The top layers press down on the bottom layers. The lower sediments are squeezed very tightly together. They become sedimentary rock.

The stripes in this rock are layers of sediments.

HOW SQUEEZING CHANGES SEDIMENTS INTO ROCK

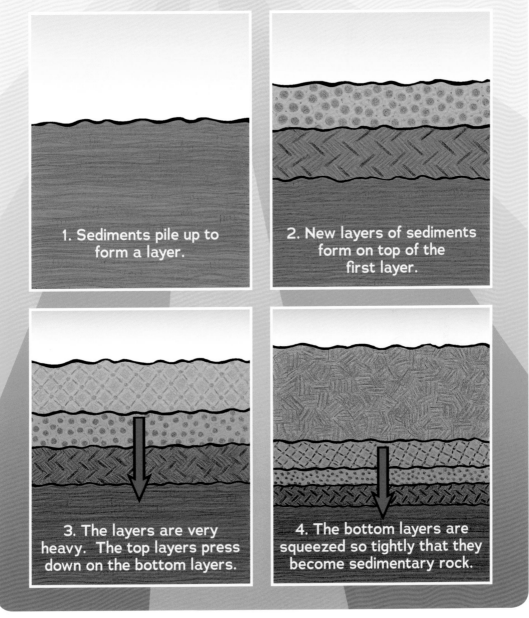

1. Sediments pile up to form a layer.

2. New layers of sediments form on top of the first layer.

3. The layers are very heavy. The top layers press down on the bottom layers.

4. The bottom layers are squeezed so tightly that they become sedimentary rock.

Sometimes loose sediments become glued tighter to make rock. This is called cementing. Cementing starts when water seeps into the spaces between the sediments. Dissolved minerals are in the water. The dissolved minerals become hard. They glue the sediments together. The cemented sediments become sedimentary rock.

This rock is called breccia. It is made of small bits of rock that have been cemented together.

Sand grains can be cemented together to form a sedimentary rock called sandstone. Conglomerate is another kind of sedimentary rock. It has a mixture of different sizes of sediments. Large pebbles, small pebbles, and sand grains are cemented together.

Conglomerate rock is made of many different sizes of sediments.

Limestone is a sedimentary rock made from shells. The shells are from animals such as clams and snails. After the animals die, their shells become sediments on the ocean bottom. Over time, they are cemented together. They become limestone.

Some of the shells in this piece of limestone have become cemented together.

Clues about a Rock's Past

Sedimentary rocks hold clues that tell where the rocks formed. Shale is a sedimentary rock made from mud. And mud is found near water. So a piece of shale may have started out as mud on a riverbank or on the bottom of a lake.

SHALE OFTEN BREAKS
INTO BIG, FLAT PIECES.

Sedimentary rock sometimes has fossils in it. Fossils are bones or other traces of animals and plants that lived long ago. Fossils of dinosaur footprints are often found in shale. Dinosaurs' feet made footprints in soft mud, just like your feet would. The mud dried and became hard.

This fossil is the bones of a dinosaur that lived millions of years ago.

The shape of the footprints was saved in the hardened mud. Over time, the sediments in the mud were cemented together. The mud turned to shale. The dinosaurs' footprints can still be seen in the rock.

Fossil dinosaur tracks show the shape of the dinosaur's feet and how it walked.

Chapter 4

METAMORPHIC ROCKS

Metamorphic rocks are the third group of rocks. Metamorphic rocks are made out of other kinds of rock. Rocks can change. A rock changes if it gets very hot but not hot enough to melt. And a rock changes if it is squeezed very, very hard. Heating and squeezing change the minerals inside the rock. The rock becomes a metamorphic rock.

This rock is called schist. Schist forms when another kind of rock changes. What can make a rock change?

Rocks that are near magma can get very hot. They do not get hot enough to melt. But the heat may change the minerals in the rocks. If the minerals change, the rocks become metamorphic rocks.

THIS ROCK WAS
SQUEEZED SO HARD
THAT ITS LAYERS BENT!

Rocks are pushed and squeezed inside Earth. Earth's crust is divided into large pieces called plates. The plates slowly move on Earth's surface. Sometimes the plates push against one another. This movement squeezes rocks tightly. Rocks that are under very deep layers of rock get squeezed too. The squeezing can change the rocks into metamorphic rock.

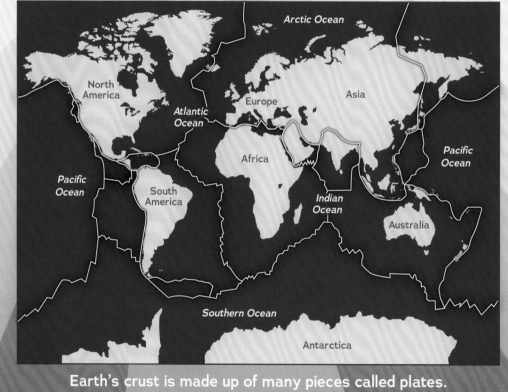

PLATES IN EARTH'S CRUST

Earth's crust is made up of many pieces called plates.
The white lines show the edges of the plates.

Marble

Limestone is a sedimentary rock. Limestone can be many colors, such as white, tan, and gray. Limestone often contains fossils of shells. When limestone gets very hot, it changes into a metamorphic rock called marble. When limestone changes into marble, the fossils in it disappear. Marble can be many different colors, such as pink, white, and black. It often has swirling lines in it.

Marble is often used to make buildings and statues.

Gneiss

Granite is an igneous rock. It is made of bits of light-colored and dark-colored minerals. The bits are all jumbled up. When granite is squeezed hard, the minerals move. They separate into light and dark layers. The granite changes into a metamorphic rock called gneiss.

Gneiss rock has many light and dark layers.

Slate

Shale is a sedimentary rock. Shale is usually gray or black. But it may be red, green, or brown. When shale is squeezed, its minerals line up in flat layers. The shale changes into a metamorphic rock called slate. Slate easily breaks apart into thin, flat pieces. Slate is usually a darker color than shale.

Slate breaks into thin, hard sheets. The sheets can be used to cover the roofs of buildings.

Chapter 5

THE ROCK CYCLE

The three groups of rocks are part of a cycle. A cycle is a pattern that happens again and again. The rock cycle changes old rocks into new ones.

Each day, the sun rises in the morning and sets in the evening. What do we call things that happen over and over?

Weathering

Water, wind, and ice change rocks. These forces scrape and scratch rocks. And they crack rocks apart. These changes are called weathering. Over millions of years, weathering can turn a mountain made of old igneous rock into sediments. The sediments can become new sedimentary rock.

Weathering made a huge hole in this rock. This has made the rock look sort of like a bridge.

Heat

Heat changes rocks too. Earth's rocky crust is always moving. Most of the movements are too slow and small for us to see. But slowly, rocks are pulled and pushed into new places. Old sedimentary and metamorphic rocks can be pushed down inside Earth. When the old rocks get hot enough, they melt. They become magma. If the magma cools and hardens, it becomes new igneous rock.

Long ago, these layers of rock were flat. Then Earth's crust moved. The layers of rock were pushed so hard that they became lifted.

Rocks All Around

Find a rock near your home or school. Look at it closely. Can you see crystals? Does the rock have pebbles in it? Try to figure out if it is an igneous rock, a sedimentary rock, or a metamorphic rock.

Rocks are everywhere. Look at the streets, buildings, and sidewalks around you. The many different rocks you see may surprise you!

A magnifying glass will help you look closely at rocks.

Glossary

cementing: gluing together

crust: Earth's outer layer

crystal: a solid shape with many flat surfaces

cycle: things happening in the same order again and again. A day's cycle is daytime changing into nighttime and back into daytime.

fossil: a bone or other trace of animals and plants that lived long ago

igneous rock: a rock formed by great heat. Many igneous rocks form deep inside Earth.

lava: melted rock on Earth's surface

magma: melted rock that is inside Earth

metamorphic rock: a rock made from other kinds of rock. Heating and squeezing can change an igneous or sedimentary rock into a metamorphic rock.

mineral: a solid substance that forms inside Earth and is not alive

plate: a large, moving piece of Earth's crust

rock cycle: the way in which old rocks are changed into new ones

sediment: a bit of mud, sand, small stone, shell or bone

sedimentary rock: a rock made from bits of mud, sand, or small stones

weathering: breaking rocks and soil into smaller pieces. Water, wind, and ice are forces that weather rocks.

Learn More about Rocks

Books

Gray, Susan H. *Geology: The Study of Rocks*. New York: Children's Press, 2012. Check out this book for a fun look at geology—the science of rocks.

Tomecek, Steve. *Everything Rocks and Minerals*. Washington, DC: National Geographic, 2010. If you like rocks, you'll love this in-depth look at rocks and minerals.

Walker, Sally M. *Marveling at Minerals*. Minneapolis: Lerner Publications Company, 2013. This book is packed with interesting information on minerals as well as beautiful photos.

Websites

If Rocks Could Talk!

http://www.amnh.org/ology/features/ifrockscouldtalk
Every rock has a story to tell about Earth's history. This website has the stories of different rocks plus photos of igneous, sedimentary, and metamorphic rocks.

Neighborhood Rocks

http://www.saltthesandbox.org/rocks/index.htm
Learn all about rock collecting! This website includes descriptions of some kinds of rocks you might find in your neighborhood.

Rocks for Kids

http://www.rocksforkids.com
This website has lots of information about rocks, including how to identify different kinds of rocks.

Index

Photo Acknowledgments

The images in this book are used with the permission of: © Marli Miller/Visuals Unlimited, Inc., pp. 4, 18; © Adam Burton/Robert Harding World Imagery/Getty Images, p. 5; © Dr. John D. Cunningham/Visuals Unlimited, Inc., p. 6; © Mark Schneider/Visuals Unlimited, Inc., p. 7; © Weldon Schloneger/Dreamstime.com, p. 8; © Ron Dahlquist/SuperStock, p. 9; © Fotosearch/Getty Images, p. 10; © Jim Sugar/CORBIS, p. 11; NOAA, p. 12; © Ken Lucas/Visuals Unlimited, Inc., p. 13; © Phil Degginger/Jack Clark Collection/Alamy, p. 14; © Wally Eberhart/Visuals Unlimited, Inc., p. 15; © Alan Majchrowicz/Peter Arnold/Getty Images, pp. 16, 17; © Photodisc/Getty Images, p. 19; © Igna Spence/Photolibrary/Getty Images, p. 20; © Laura Westlund/Independent Picture Service, pp. 21, 30; © Scientifica/Visuals Unlimited, Inc., pp. 22, 28; © Peter Walton Photography/Photolibrary/Getty Images, p. 23; © Charles D. Winters/Photo Researchers, Inc., p. 24; © Gary Ombler/Dorling Kindersley/Getty Images, p. 25; © Heinrich van den Berg/Gallo Images/Getty Images, p. 26; © Minden Pictures/SuperStock, p. 27; © Ferrell McCollough/Visuals Unlimited, Inc., p. 29; © PjrTravel/Alamy, p. 31; © Andrew J. Martinez/Photo Researchers, Inc., p. 32; © Science VU/Visuals Unlimited, Inc., p. 33; © iStockphoto.com/James Brey, p. 34; USGS, p. 35; © Inga Spence/Visuals Unlimited, Inc., p. 36; © Spencer Grant/Photo Researchers, Inc., p. 37. Front cover: © Kathy Libby/Bigstock.com.

Main body text set in Adrianna Regular 14/20.
Typeface provided by Chank.